Sushi Cookbook

Mouthwatering Sushi Recipes for The Amateur Cook!

BY: Valeria Ray

License Notes

Copyright © 2019 Valeria Ray All Rights Reserved

All rights to the content of this book are reserved by the Author without exception unless permission is given stating otherwise.

The Author have no claims as to the authenticity of the content and the Reader bears all responsibility and risk when following the content. The Author is not liable for any reparations, damages, accidents, injuries or other incidents occurring from the Reader following all or part of this publication.

Table of Contents

Introduction 6

    Sake Sushi Nori 8

    Spicy Tuna Roll 12

    Shrimp (Ebi) Tail Sushi 16

    Spicy Tuna Rice Bowl 19

    Dragon Roll 21

    Tuna Tataki 25

    Shoyu 'Ahi Poke 28

    Tako (Octopus) Sushi Roll 30

    Scallop Sushi 33

    Rainbow Sushi 36

    Fried Shrimp Rolls 40

    California Sushi Cone 43

    Philadelphia Roll 46

Tuna (Maguro) Sushi 49

Mackerel (Saba) Sushi 52

Horse Mackerel (Aji) Sushi 55

Whale Meat Sushi 58

Vegetarian Sushi Rice Bowl 61

California Sushi Bowl 63

Sea Urchin Sushi 65

Puffer Fish Sushi 68

California Roll 71

Fatty Tuna Sushi 75

Boston Roll 78

Yellowtail Sushi 81

Seattle Roll 84

Salmon Sushi Bowl 87

Salmon & Wasabi Sushi Bowl 89

Deconstructed Sushi Salad Bowl 91

Spicy California Sushi Salad... 93

Conclusion.. 95

About the Author... 96

Author's Afterthoughts.. 98

Introduction

Sushi, simply put is any dish that is composed of Sushi rice, along with vegetables, seafood or a combination of the two. Contrary to popular belief, Sushi does not mean raw fish. It is the rice component of the dish and is a special type of Japanese rice. The raw fish component of the Sushi meal is called Sashimi.

The term Sashimi can also be used when referring to very fresh raw meat that is thinly sliced. When this Sushi rice is covered with seaweed (also called Nori in Japan) then wrapped in a roll, we get what we enjoy to eat, a Sushi roll. There are tons of varieties that we can achieve by simply mix and matching vegetables, fish and even meats in some cases to get delicious Sushi varieties, and luckily, we are and to explore as many of them as we can. Enough chitter chatter, let's jump in and make some Sushi rolls.

Sake Sushi Nori

Sake, the Japanese name for Salmon, is a popular Sashimi fish used in Sushi rolls.

Ingredients:

- Cooked Sushi Rice (1½ cups)
- Fresh Salmon (4 oz., sashimi grade, thinly sliced lengthwise)
- Cucumber (4oz, diced)
- Avocado (4oz, thinly sliced)
- Fresh Crab Meat (4oz., sashimi grade, diced)
- Sesame Oil (1/2 tsp.)
- Nori (1 sheet, halved)
- Sesame Seeds (2 tbsp.)
- Special Equipment/Tools Needed:
- Bamboo Mat
- Plastic Wrap (to cover bamboo mat)
- Tezu (mixture of 2 tsp. rice vinegar and ¼ cup water)

Directions:

1. Combine crab meat, cucumber, and sesame oil in a medium bowl.

2. Cover your bamboo mat with plastic wrap; then lay it on a flat surface.

3. Layer your flat sliced salmon on the bottom edge of the mat.

4. Place your nori on your mat, starting on top of the salmon slice with the silkier side facing down.

5. Top with ¾ cup of your Sushi rice. Carefully wet your fingertips in tezu then proceed to spread the rice evenly over the nori. Once spread evenly sprinkle with sesame seeds.

6. Gently flip your sheet of nori over so that the rice is left flat on the salmon and bamboo mat.

7. Line up the edge of your nori sheet and salmon with the bamboo mat then spread your salmon mixture at the bottom end of the nori, then top your filling with avocado slices.

8. Placing your index and middle fingers in front of your tuna filling, position your thumbs below the bamboo mat and roll the mat over to form a tight cylinder.

9. Begin to roll the mat into tight cylindrical shapes keeping a gentle pressure on the mat. Roll until at the end.

10. When you have reached the end of your nori sheet, release the mat and lift the Sushi roll off the mat gently.

11. Using a clean, sharp knife, cut the roll into 6 equal pieces. Clean your knife after each slice.

12. Remove plastic wrap and Enjoy!

Spicy Tuna Roll

A spicy combination of fresh tuna, nori, and Sushi rice.

Yields: 8 pieces

Time: 30 minutes

Ingredients:

- Cooked Sushi Rice (1½ cups)
- Fresh Tuna (4 oz., sashimi grade, minced)
- Sriracha Sauce (3 tsp.)
- Green Onion (1 tsp, chopped)
- Sesame Oil (1/2 tsp.)
- Nori (1 sheet, halved)
- Sesame Seeds (2 tbsp.)
- Spicy Mayo (optional for garnish/dipping)
- Special Equipment/Tools Needed:
- Bamboo Mat
- Plastic Wrap (to cover bamboo mat)
- Tezu (mixture of rice vinegar - 2 tsp. and ¼ cup water)

Directions:

1. Combine minced tuna, green onions, sesame oil, and sriracha sauce.

2. Cover your bamboo mat with plastic wrap; then lay it on a flat surface.

3. Place your nori on your bamboo mat with the silkier side facing down.

4. Top with ¾ cup of your Sushi rice. Carefully wet your fingertips in tezu then proceed to spread the rice over the nori. Once spread evenly sprinkle with sesame seeds.

5. Gently flip your sheet of nori so that the rice is left flat on the bamboo mat.

6. Line up the edge of your nori sheet and the bamboo mat then spread your tuna mixture towards the bottom edge of the nori.

7. Placing your index and middle fingers in front of your tuna filling, position your thumbs below the bamboo mat and roll the mat over to form a tight cylinder.

8. Begin to roll the mat into tight cylindrical shapes keeping a gentle pressure on the mat. Roll until at the end.

9. When you have reached the end of your nori sheet, release the mat and lift the Sushi roll off the mat gently.

10. Using a clean, sharp knife, cut the roll into 6 equal pieces. Clean your knife after each slice.

11. Remove plastic wrap and Enjoy!

Shrimp (Ebi) Tail Sushi

Shrimp lovers will absolute love this roll!

Yields: 6 Pieces

Time Needed: 30 min

Ingredients:

- Cooked Sushi Rice (1½ cups)
- Fresh Shrimp Tail Meat (6 oz., large, seasoned with salt and lemon zest)
- Sesame Oil (2 tbsp.)
- Special Equipment/Tools Needed:
- Bamboo Mat
- Plastic Wrap (to cover bamboo mat)
- Tezu (mixture of 2 tsp. rice vinegar and ¼ cup water)

Directions:

1. Cover your bamboo mat with plastic wrap; then lay it on a flat surface.

2. Line up the edge of your bamboo mat with your shrimp tails in a straight line down the edge of your mat.

3. Top with 1 cup of your Sushi rice. Carefully wet your fingertips in tezu then proceed to spread the rice evenly over the shrimp, and the mat. Once spread evenly sprinkle with sesame seeds.

4. Position your thumbs below the bamboo mat and roll the mat over to form a tight cylinder.

5. Begin to roll the mat into tight cylindrical shapes keeping a gentle pressure on the mat. Roll until at the end.

6. When you have reached the end of your roll, release the mat and lift the Sushi roll off the mat gently.

7. Using a clean, sharp knife, cut the roll into 6 equal pieces. Clean your knife after each slice.

8. Remove plastic wrap and Enjoy!

Spicy Tuna Rice Bowl

All the pleasures of a spicy tuna roll in a bowl.

Ingredients:

- Cooked Sushi Rice (1½ cups)
- Fresh Tuna (4 oz., sashimi grade, minced)
- Avocado (1/2, sliced)
- Cucumber (4oz, fine julienne)
- Carrot (4oz., fine julienne)
- Green Onion (1 tsp, chopped)
- Sesame Oil (1/2 tsp.)
- Sesame Seeds (2 tbsp.)
- Spicy Mayo (For use as a sauce)

Directions:

1. Split your Sushi rice into 2 medium bowls.

2. Top with your tuna, cucumber, carrot, and green onion.

3. Sprinkle with sesame seeds

4. Top tuna with spicy mayo.

5. Serve and enjoy!

Dragon Roll

A tasty combination of eel, cucumber, and avocado.

Yields: 6 pieces

Time: 30 minutes

Ingredients:

- Cooked Sushi Rice (1½ cups)
- Fresh Eel (4 oz., sashimi grade, thinly sliced lengthwise)
- Cucumber (4oz, diced)
- Avocado (4oz, thinly sliced)
- Caviar (2oz.)
- Sesame Oil (1/2 tsp.)
- Nori (1 sheet, halved)
- Sesame Seeds (2 tbsp.)
- Special Equipment/Tools Needed:
- Bamboo Mat
- Plastic Wrap (to cover bamboo mat)
- Tezu (mixture of 2 tsp. rice vinegar and ¼ cup water)

Directions:

1. Combine eel, cucumber, and sesame oil in a medium bowl.

2. Cover your bamboo mat with plastic wrap; then lay it on a flat surface.

3. Layer your avocado slices on the bottom edge of the mat.

4. Place your nori on your mat, starting on top of the salmon slice with the silkier side facing down.

5. Top with ¾ cup of your Sushi rice. Carefully wet your fingertips in tezu then proceed to spread the rice evenly over the nori. Once spread evenly sprinkle with sesame seeds.

6. Gently flip your sheet of nori over so that the rice is left flat on the salmon and bamboo mat.

7. Line up the edge of your nori sheet and avocado with the bamboo mat then spread your eel mixture at the bottom end of the nori, then top your filling with drippings of caviar.

8. Placing your index and middle fingers in front of your filling, position your thumbs below the bamboo mat and roll the mat over to form a tight cylinder.

9. Begin to roll the mat into tight cylindrical shapes keeping a gentle pressure on the mat. Roll until at the end.

10. When you have reached the end of your nori sheet, release the mat and lift the Sushi roll off the mat gently.

11. Using a clean, sharp knife, cut the roll into 6 equal pieces. Clean your knife after each slice.

12. Remove plastic wrap and Enjoy!

Tuna Tataki

Ponzu, a citrus-flavored soy sauce, is a main ingredient in this light recipe and gives it an uplifting flavor.

Yield: Serves 2

Preparation Time: 25 minutes

Ingredients:

- 2 tablespoons cooking oil
- ½ pound tuna
- 3 tablespoons ponzu
- 2 teaspoons sesame oil
- 1 teaspoon soy sauce
- 1 scallion, thinly sliced
- 1 teaspoon fresh ginger, grated
- 1 teaspoon sesame seeds
- Pinch cracked black pepper
- Lemon slices for garnish

Directions:

1. Combine the ponzu, sesame oil and soy sauce together. Stir in the grated ginger, sesame seeds, cracked black pepper and sliced scallions. This is the dressing that you will be pouring over the fish in a later step.

2. Add the oil to a pan and heat on the stove until hot. Carefully add the tuna, searing the fish on all sides.

3. Remove the tuna carefully from the pan and thinly slice the fish. Place the fish on the serving plates.

4. Carefully pour the dressing made in Step 1 over the sliced tuna. Garnish with lemon slices if desired.

Shoyu 'Ahi Poke

Poke literally translates to "section" or "to slice or cut," so it makes sense that it's the name of a dish that's basically just cubes of beautiful raw fish. The most common type of fish used is 'ahi, or yellowfin tuna, but no matter what, you want the freshest fish you can possibly find.

Total Time: 10m

Servings: 2 to 4

Ingredients:

- 1 lb. fresh 'ahi steak, cold - diced into small cubes
- 1½ tbsp. soy sauce
- 1 tbsp sesame oil
- ¾ tsp salt,
- ¼ cup thinly yellow onion
- ½ cup chopped green onions
- 1 tbsp toasted macadamia nuts, finely chopped
- 2 cups plain rice, for serving

Directions:

1. Combine all the ingredients except the rice. Season to taste.

2. Serve over the rice!

Tako (Octopus) Sushi Roll

A brilliant combination of Tako, the Japanese term for Octopus, and Sushi Rice.

Yields: 6 Pieces

Time: 30 min

Ingredients:

- Cooked Sushi Rice (1½ cups)
- Fresh Tako/Octopus (4 oz., sashimi grade, thinly sliced lengthwise)
- Perilla Leaves (12 leaves, washed)
- Sesame Oil (1/2 tsp.)
- Special Equipment/Tools Needed:
- Bamboo Mat
- Plastic Wrap (to cover bamboo mat)
- Tezu (mixture of 2 tsp. rice vinegar and ¼ cup water)

Directions:

Cover your bamboo mat with plastic wrap; then lay it on a flat surface.

Layer your thinly sliced Octopus on the bottom edge of the mat.

Top your Octopus with Perilla leaves and brush the leaf and octopus with sesame oil.

Follow the leaves with a ¾ cup of your Sushi rice. Carefully wet your fingertips in tezu then proceed to spread the rice evenly over the mat.

Line up the edge of your Sushi rice with the bamboo mat then position your thumbs below the bamboo mat and roll the mat over to form a tight cylinder.

Begin to roll the mat into tight cylindrical shapes keeping a gentle pressure on the mat. Roll until at the end.

When you have reached the end of your roll, release the mat and lift the Sushi roll off the mat gently.

Using a clean, sharp knife, cut the roll into 6 equal pieces. Clean your knife after each slice.

Remove plastic wrap and Enjoy!

Scallop Sushi

The delicacies of a scallop paired with the velocity of Sushi rice.

Yields: 6

Time: 30 minutes

Ingredients:

- Cooked Sushi Rice (1½ cups)
- Fresh Scallop (6 oz., large thinly sliced)
- Sesame Oil (2 tbsp.)
- Special Equipment/Tools Needed:
- Bamboo Mat
- Plastic Wrap (to cover bamboo mat)
- Tezu (mixture of 2 tsp. rice vinegar and ¼ cup water)

Directions:

Cover your bamboo mat with plastic wrap; then lay it on a flat surface.

Line up the edge of your bamboo mat with your scallop in a straight line down the edge of your mat.

Top with 1 cup of your Sushi rice. Carefully wet your fingertips in tezu then proceed to spread the rice evenly over the scallop, and the mat. Once spread evenly sprinkle with sesame seeds.

Position your thumbs below the bamboo mat and roll the mat over to form a tight cylinder.

Begin to roll the mat into tight cylindrical shapes keeping a gentle pressure on the mat. Roll until at the end.

When you have reached the end of your roll, release the mat and lift the Sushi roll off the mat gently.

Using a clean, sharp knife, cut the roll into 6 equal pieces. Clean your knife after each slice.

Remove plastic wrap and Enjoy!

Rainbow Sushi

A colorful burst of deliciousness that you just can't help but admire while you eat.

Yields: 6 Pieces

Time: 30 minutes

Ingredients:

- Cooked Sushi Rice (1½ cups)
- Fresh Salmon (4 oz., sashimi grade, thinly sliced lengthwise)
- Fresh Ahi Tuna (4 oz., sashimi grade, thinly sliced lengthwise)
- Cucumber (4oz, diced)
- Avocado (4oz, thinly sliced)
- Fresh Crab Meat (4oz., sashimi grade, minced)
- Sesame Oil (1/2 tsp.)
- Sriracha Sauce (3 tsp.)
- Nori (1 sheet, halved)
- Sesame Seeds (2 tbsp.)

Special Equipment/Tools Needed:

- Bamboo Mat
- Plastic Wrap (to cover bamboo mat)
- Tezu (mixture of 2 tsp. rice vinegar and ¼ cup water)

Directions:

Combine crab meat, cucumber, sriracha sauce, and sesame oil in a medium bowl.

Cover your bamboo mat with plastic wrap; then lay it on a flat surface.

Layer your flat sliced salmon, ahi tuna, and avocado on the bottom edge of the mat alternately.

Place your nori on your mat, starting on top of the sashimi and avocado slices with the silkier side facing down.

Top with ¾ cup of your Sushi rice. Carefully wet your fingertips in tezu then proceed to spread the rice evenly over the nori. Once spread evenly sprinkle with sesame seeds.

Gently flip your sheet of nori over so that the rice is left flat on the sashimi and bamboo mat.

Line up the edge of your nori sheet and sashimi with the bamboo mat then spread your crab mixture at the bottom end of the nori.

Placing your index and middle fingers in front of your filling, position your thumbs below the bamboo mat and roll the mat over to form a tight cylinder.

Begin to roll the mat into tight cylindrical shapes keeping a gentle pressure on the mat. Roll until at the end.

When you have reached the end of your nori sheet, release the mat and lift the Sushi roll off the mat gently.

Using a clean, sharp knife, cut the roll into 6 equal pieces. Clean your knife after each slice.

Remove plastic wrap and Enjoy!

Fried Shrimp Rolls

The magical combination of fried shrimp, avocado, and Sushi rice.

Yields: 6 Pieces

Time: 30 minutes

Ingredients:

- Cooked Sushi Rice (1½ cups)
- Shrimp (4 oz., diced, fried)
- Avocado (1, sliced in ½ inch slices)
- Salt (2 tsp.)
- Sesame Oil (1/2 tsp.)
- Nori (1 sheet, halved)
- Sesame Seeds (2 tbsp.)

Special Equipment/Tools Needed:

- Bamboo Mat
- Plastic Wrap (to cover bamboo mat)
- Tezu (mixture of 2 tsp. rice vinegar and ¼ cup water)

Directions:

Combine fried shrimp, sesame oil, and salt in a medium bowl.

Cover your bamboo mat with plastic wrap; then lay it on a flat surface.

Place your nori on your bamboo mat with the silkier side facing down.

Top with ¾ cup of your Sushi rice. Carefully wet your fingertips in tezu then proceed to spread the rice evenly over the nori. Once spread evenly sprinkle with sesame seeds.

Line up the edge of your nori sheet and the bamboo mat then spread your shrimp mixture at the bottom end of the rice then top with avocado slices.

Placing your index and middle fingers in front of your filling to hold it in, position your thumbs under the bamboo mat and roll the mat over to form a tight cylinder.

Begin to roll the mat into tight cylindrical shapes keeping a gentle pressure on the mat. Roll until at the end.

When you have reached the end of your roll, release the mat and lift the Sushi roll off the mat gently.

Using a clean, sharp knife, cut the roll into 6 equal pieces. Clean your knife after each slice.

Remove plastic wrap and Enjoy!

California Sushi Cone

A sushi meal that you can hold in your hand.

Yields: 3 cones

Time Needed: 30 minutes

Ingredients:

- Cooked Sushi Rice (1 cups)
- Shiso Leaves (6)
- Japanese Cucumber (1, seeded, and julienned)
- Avocado (1/2, thinly sliced)
- Crab Meat (1 Cup, shredded)
- Nori (3 sheets)
- Kewpie Mayo (2 tbsp.)
- Tobiko (1 tbsp.)
- Sesame Seeds (to sprinkle for garnish)

Directions:

Place your nori on a flat surface with the silkier side facing down.

Top with 4 tablespoons of your Sushi rice. Carefully wet your fingertips in tezu then proceed to spread the rice evenly over the left side of the nori sheet. Once spread evenly sprinkle with sesame seeds.

Top with two Shiso leaves on a bias, followed by some cucumber, crab, a slice of avocado, and a teaspoon of kewpie mayo.

Placing your index and middle fingers in front of your filling to hold it in, position your thumbs below the nori sheet and roll the nori from the left-hand corner to the top right end forming a cone.

Use a grain of rice to stick your nori together.

Top with Tobiko, and sesame seeds

Repeat with all three sheets.

Serve and Enjoy!

Philadelphia Roll

A dazzling combination of salmon and cream cheese.

Yields: 6

Time: 30 minutes

Ingredients:

- Cooked Sushi Rice (1½ cups)
- Cucumber (4 oz., diced)
- Avocado (1/2, diced)
- Fresh Salmon (4oz., diced)
- Onion (1, small, chopped)
- Cream Cheese (1/4 cup., diced)
- Nori (1 sheet, halved)
- Sesame Seeds (2 tbsp.)
- Special Equipment/Tools Needed:
- Bamboo Mat
- Plastic Wrap (to cover bamboo mat)
- Tezu (mixture of 2 tsp. rice vinegar and ¼ cup water)

Directions:

Combine salmon, cucumber, avocado, onion, and cream cheese in a medium bowl.

Cover your bamboo mat with plastic wrap; then lay it on a flat surface.

Place your nori on your bamboo mat with the silkier side facing down.

Top with ¾ cup of your Sushi rice. Carefully wet your fingertips in tezu then proceed to spread the rice evenly over the nori. Once spread evenly sprinkle with sesame seeds.

Line up the edge of your nori sheet and the bamboo mat then spread your salmon mix at the bottom end of the nori.

Placing your index and middle fingers in front of your filling to hold it in, position your thumbs under the bamboo mat and roll the mat over to form a tight cylinder.

Begin to roll the mat into tight cylindrical shapes keeping a gentle pressure on the mat. Roll until at the end.

When you have reached the end of your nori sheet, release the mat and lift the Sushi roll off the mat gently.

Using a clean, sharp knife, cut the roll into 6 equal pieces. Clean your knife after each slice.

Remove plastic wrap and Enjoy!

Tuna (Maguro) Sushi

There's nothing tastier than a fresh slice of tuna paired with Sushi rice.

Yields: 6 Pieces

Time: 30 Minutes

Ingredients:

- Cooked Sushi Rice (1½ cups)
- Fresh Tuna Meat (6 oz., large, sashimi grade, thinly sliced)
- Sesame Oil (2 tbsp.)
- Special Equipment/Tools Needed:
- Bamboo Mat
- Plastic Wrap (to cover bamboo mat)
- Tezu (mixture of 2 tsp. rice vinegar and ¼ cup water)

Directions:

Cover your bamboo mat with plastic wrap; then lay it on a flat surface.

Line up the edge of your bamboo mat with your tuna in a straight line down the edge of your mat.

Top with 1 cup of your Sushi rice. Carefully wet your fingertips in tezu then proceed to spread the rice evenly over the tuna, and the mat. Once spread evenly sprinkle with sesame seeds.

Position your thumbs below the bamboo mat and roll the mat over to form a tight cylinder.

Begin to roll the mat into tight cylindrical shapes keeping a gentle pressure on the mat. Roll until at the end.

When you have reached the end of your roll, release the mat and lift the Sushi roll off the mat gently.

Using a clean, sharp knife, cut the roll into 6 equal pieces. Clean your knife after each slice.

Remove plastic wrap and Enjoy!

Mackerel (Saba) Sushi

That's right! Mackerel can, in fact, be used to make sushi. Here's a delicious recipe showing how.

Yields: 6 pieces

Time: 30 minutes

Ingredients:

- Cooked Sushi Rice (1½ cups)
- Fresh Mackerel Meat (6 oz., large, sashimi grade, thinly sliced)
- Sesame Oil (2 tbsp.)
- Special Equipment/Tools Needed:
- Bamboo Mat
- Plastic Wrap (to cover bamboo mat)
- Tezu (mixture of 2 tsp. rice vinegar and ¼ cup water)

Directions:

Cover your bamboo mat with plastic wrap; then lay it on a flat surface.

Line up the edge of your bamboo mat with your mackerel in a straight line down the edge of your mat.

Top with 1 cup of your Sushi rice. Carefully wet your fingertips in tezu then proceed to spread the rice evenly over the mackerel, and the mat. Once spread evenly sprinkle with sesame seeds.

Position your thumbs below the bamboo mat and roll the mat over to form a tight cylinder.

Begin to roll the mat into tight cylindrical shapes keeping a gentle pressure on the mat. Roll until at the end.

When you have reached the end of your roll, release the mat and lift the Sushi roll off the mat gently.

Using a clean, sharp knife, cut the roll into 6 equal pieces. Clean your knife after each slice.

Remove plastic wrap and Enjoy!

Horse Mackerel (Aji) Sushi

A delicious fish from the Atlantic, that when eaten at its freshest peak is utterly delicious.

Yields 6 pieces

Time: 30 Minutes

Ingredients:

- Cooked Sushi Rice (1½ cups)
- Fresh Horse Mackerel Meat (6 oz., large, sashimi grade, thinly sliced)
- Sesame Oil (2 tbsp.)
- Special Equipment/Tools Needed:
- Bamboo Mat
- Plastic Wrap (to cover bamboo mat)
- Tezu (mixture of 2 tsp. rice vinegar and ¼ cup water)

Directions:

Cover your bamboo mat with plastic wrap; then lay it on a flat surface.

Line up the edge of your bamboo mat with your mackerel in a straight line down the edge of your mat.

Top with 1 cup of your Sushi rice. Carefully wet your fingertips in tezu then proceed to spread the rice evenly over the mackerel, and the mat. Once spread evenly sprinkle with sesame seeds.

Position your thumbs below the bamboo mat and roll the mat over to form a tight cylinder.

Begin to roll the mat into tight cylindrical shapes keeping a gentle pressure on the mat. Roll until at the end.

When you have reached the end of your roll, release the mat and lift the Sushi roll off the mat gently.

Using a clean, sharp knife, cut the roll into 6 equal pieces. Clean your knife after each slice.

Remove plastic wrap and Enjoy!

Whale Meat Sushi

A delicious, yet exotic sushi roll.

Yields: 6 pieces

Time: 30 Minutes

Ingredients:

- Cooked Sushi Rice (1½ cups)
- Fresh Whale Meat (6 oz., thinly sliced)
- Sesame Oil (2 tbsp.)
- Special Equipment/Tools Needed:
- Bamboo Mat
- Plastic Wrap (to cover bamboo mat)
- Tezu (mixture of 2 tsp. rice vinegar and ¼ cup water)

Directions:

Cover your bamboo mat with plastic wrap; then lay it on a flat surface.

Line up the edge of your bamboo mat with your whale meat in a straight line down the edge of your mat.

Top with 1 cup of your Sushi rice. Carefully wet your fingertips in tezu then proceed to spread the rice evenly over the whale meat, and the mat. Once spread evenly sprinkle with sesame seeds.

Position your thumbs below the bamboo mat and roll the mat over to form a tight cylinder.

Begin to roll the mat into tight cylindrical shapes keeping a gentle pressure on the mat. Roll until at the end.

When you have reached the end of your roll, release the mat and lift the Sushi roll off the mat gently.

Using a clean, sharp knife, cut the roll into 6 equal pieces. Clean your knife after each slice.

Remove plastic wrap and Enjoy!

Vegetarian Sushi Rice Bowl

This recipe is just as it sounds; it allows you to enjoy all the goodness of a sushi roll in a bowl.

Yields: 2 Servings

Time Needed: 15 Minutes

Ingredients:

- Cooked Sushi Rice (1½ cups)
- Cucumber (4 oz., julienne)
- Carrot (4 oz., julienne)
- Avocado (1/2, diced)
- Nori (1 sheet, minced)
- Sesame Seeds (2 tbsp.)

Directions:

Split your Sushi rice into 2 medium bowls.

Mix in your minced nori

Top with your cucumber, avocado, and carrot.

Sprinkle with sesame seeds

Serve and enjoy!

California Sushi Bowl

A California roll in a bowl!

Yields: 2 Servings

Time: 15 minutes

Ingredients:

- Cooked Sushi Rice (1½ cups)
- Fresh Crab Meat (1 can season with salt and lemon zest)
- Avocado (1, cut into ½ inch slices)
- Cucumber (1, cut into ½ inch slices)
- Sesame Seeds (2 tbsp.)

Directions:

Split your Sushi rice into 2 medium bowls.

Top with your crab meat, cucumber, and avocado.

Sprinkle with sesame seeds

Serve and enjoy!

Sea Urchin Sushi

A new and interesting way to enjoy sea urchin.

Yields: 6 pieces

Time: 30 minutes

Ingredients:

- Cooked Sushi Rice (1½ cups)
- Fresh Sea Urchin (6 oz., thinly sliced)
- Sesame Oil (2 tbsp.)
- Special Equipment/Tools Needed:
- Bamboo Mat
- Plastic Wrap (to cover bamboo mat)
- Tezu (mixture of 2 tsp. rice vinegar and ¼ cup water)

Directions:

Cover your bamboo mat with plastic wrap; then lay it on a flat surface.

Line up the edge of your bamboo mat with your sea urchin in a straight line down the edge of your mat.

Top with 1 cup of your Sushi rice. Carefully wet your fingertips in tezu then proceed to spread the rice evenly over the sea urchin, and the mat. Once spread evenly sprinkle with sesame seeds.

Position your thumbs below the bamboo mat and roll the mat over to form a tight cylinder.

Begin to roll the mat into tight cylindrical shapes keeping a gentle pressure on the mat. Roll until at the end.

When you have reached the end of your roll, release the mat and lift the Sushi roll off the mat gently.

Using a clean, sharp knife, cut the roll into 6 equal pieces. Clean your knife after each slice.

Remove plastic wrap and Enjoy!

Puffer Fish Sushi

Again, another exotic dish that can be easily prepared.

Yields: 6 pieces

Time: 30 minutes

Ingredients:

- Cooked Sushi Rice (1½ cups)
- Fresh Pufferfish (6 oz., large thinly sliced)
- Sesame Oil (2 tbsp.)
- Special Equipment/Tools Needed:
- Bamboo Mat
- Plastic Wrap (to cover bamboo mat)
- Tezu (mixture of 2 tsp. rice vinegar and ¼ cup water)

Directions:

Cover your bamboo mat with plastic wrap; then lay it on a flat surface.

Line up the edge of your bamboo mat with your puffer fish in a straight line down the edge of your mat.

Top with 1 cup of your Sushi rice. Carefully wet your fingertips in tezu then proceed to spread the rice evenly over the puffer fish, and the mat. Once spread evenly sprinkle with sesame seeds.

Position your thumbs below the bamboo mat and roll the mat over to form a tight cylinder.

Begin to roll the mat into tight cylindrical shapes keeping a gentle pressure on the mat. Roll until at the end.

When you have reached the end of your roll, release the mat and lift the Sushi roll off the mat gently.

Using a clean, sharp knife, cut the roll into 6 equal pieces. Clean your knife after each slice.

Remove plastic wrap and Enjoy!

California Roll

A deliciously popular sushi roll and an absolute crowd pleaser!

Yields: 8 pieces

Time Needed: 30 minutes

Ingredients:

- Cooked Sushi Rice (1½ cups)
- Fresh Crab Meat (1 can season with salt and lemon zest)
- Nori (2 sheets, roasted, halved)
- Avocado (1, cut into ½ inch slices)
- Cucumber (1, cut into ½ inch slices)
- Sesame Seeds (2 tbsp.)
- Special Equipment/Tools Needed:
- Bamboo Mat
- Plastic Wrap (to cover bamboo mat)
- Tezu (mixture of 2 tsp. rice vinegar and ¼ cup water)

Directions:

Cover your bamboo mat with plastic wrap; then lay it on a flat surface.

Place your nori on your bamboo mat with the silkier side facing down.

Top with 1 cup of your Sushi rice. Carefully wet your fingertips in tezu then proceed to spread the rice evenly over the nori. Once spread evenly sprinkle with sesame seeds.

Gently flip your sheet of nori over so that the rice is left flat on the bamboo mat.

Line up the edge of your nori sheet and the bamboo mat then spread your crab mix at the bottom end of the nori then layer with avocado and cucumber.

Placing your index and middle fingers in front of your filling, position your thumbs below the bamboo mat and roll the mat over to form a tight cylinder.

Begin to roll the mat into tight cylindrical shapes keeping a gentle pressure on the mat. Roll until at the end.

When you have reached the end of your nori sheet, release the mat and lift the Sushi roll off the mat gently.

Using a clean, sharp knife, cut the roll into 8 equal pieces. Clean your knife after each slice.

Remove plastic wrap and Enjoy!

Fatty Tuna Sushi

Indulge in the smooth, silky pleasure of fatty tuna, alongside Sushi rice.

Yields: 6 pieces

Time: 30 minutes

Ingredients:

- Cooked Sushi Rice (1½ cups)
- Fresh Otorro Tuna Meat (6 oz., large, sashimi grade, thinly sliced)
- Sesame Oil (2 tbsp.)
- Special Equipment/Tools Needed:
- Bamboo Mat
- Plastic Wrap (to cover bamboo mat)
- Tezu (mixture of 2 tsp. rice vinegar and ¼ cup water)

Directions:

Cover your bamboo mat with plastic wrap; then lay it on a flat surface.

Line up the edge of your bamboo mat with your tuna in a straight line down the edge of your mat.

Top with 1 cup of your Sushi rice. Carefully wet your fingertips in tezu then proceed to spread the rice evenly over the tuna, and the mat. Once spread evenly sprinkle with sesame seeds.

Position your thumbs below the bamboo mat and roll the mat over to form a tight cylinder.

Begin to roll the mat into tight cylindrical shapes keeping a gentle pressure on the mat. Roll until at the end.

When you have reached the end of your roll, release the mat and lift the Sushi roll off the mat gently.

Using a clean, sharp knife, cut the roll into 6 equal pieces. Clean your knife after each slice.

Remove plastic wrap and Enjoy!

Boston Roll

Much like a California roll, but made with poached shrimp instead of crab.

Yields: 6

Time: 30 minutes

Ingredients:

- Cooked Sushi Rice (1½ cups)
- Shrimp meat (6 oz., poached)
- Nori (2 sheets, roasted, halved)
- Avocado (1, cut into ½ inch slices)
- Cucumber (1, cut into ½ inch slices)
- Sesame Seeds (2 tbsp.)
- Special Equipment/Tools Needed:
- Bamboo Mat
- Plastic Wrap (to cover bamboo mat)
- Tezu (mixture of 2 tsp. rice vinegar and ¼ cup water)

Directions:

Cover your bamboo mat with plastic wrap; then lay it on a flat surface.

Place your nori on your bamboo mat with the silkier side facing down.

Top with 1 cup of your Sushi rice. Carefully wet your fingertips in tezu then proceed to spread the rice evenly over the nori. Once spread evenly sprinkle with sesame seeds.

Gently flip your sheet of nori over so that the rice is left flat on the bamboo mat.

Line up the edge of your nori sheet and the bamboo mat then spread your poached shrimp at the bottom end of the nori then layer with avocado and cucumber.

Placing your index and middle fingers in front of your filling, position your thumbs below the bamboo mat and roll the mat over to form a tight cylinder.

Begin to roll the mat into tight cylindrical shapes keeping a gentle pressure on the mat. Roll until at the end.

When you have reached the end of your nori sheet, release the mat and lift the Sushi roll off the mat gently.

Using a clean, sharp knife, cut the roll into 8 equal pieces. Clean your knife after each slice.

Remove plastic wrap and Enjoy!

Yellowtail Sushi

Sushi rice topped with delicate yellowtail.

Yields: 6

Time: 30 minutes

Ingredients:

- Cooked Sushi Rice (1½ cups)
- Fresh Yellowtail (6 oz., thinly sliced)
- Sesame Oil (2 tbsp.)
- Special Equipment/Tools Needed:
- Bamboo Mat
- Plastic Wrap (to cover bamboo mat)
- Tezu (mixture of 2 tsp. rice vinegar and ¼ cup water)

Directions:

Cover your bamboo mat with plastic wrap; then lay it on a flat surface.

Line up the edge of your bamboo mat with your yellowtail in a straight line down the edge of your mat.

Top with 1 cup of your Sushi rice. Carefully wet your fingertips in tezu then proceed to spread the rice evenly over the yellowtail, and the mat. Once spread evenly sprinkle with sesame seeds.

Position your thumbs below the bamboo mat and roll the mat over to form a tight cylinder.

Begin to roll the mat into tight cylindrical shapes keeping a gentle pressure on the mat. Roll until at the end.

When you have reached the end of your roll, release the mat and lift the Sushi roll off the mat gently.

Using a clean, sharp knife, cut the roll into 6 equal pieces. Clean your knife after each slice.

Remove plastic wrap and Enjoy!

Seattle Roll

A delicious combination of cucumber, cream cheese, salmon, and avocado.

Yields: 6 pieces

Time: 30 minutes

Ingredients:

- Cooked Sushi Rice (1½ cups)
- Cucumber (4 oz., diced)
- Avocado (1/2, diced)
- Fresh Salmon (4oz., diced)
- Cream Cheese (2 tbsp., chopped)
- Nori (1 sheet, halved)
- Sesame Seeds (2 tbsp.)
- Special Equipment/Tools Needed:
- Bamboo Mat
- Plastic Wrap (to cover bamboo mat)
- Tezu (mixture of 2 tsp. rice vinegar and ¼ cup water)

Directions:

Combine salmon, cucumber, avocado, and cream cheese in a medium bowl.

Cover your bamboo mat with plastic wrap; then lay it on a flat surface.

Place your nori on your bamboo mat with the silkier side facing down.

Top with ¾ cup of your Sushi rice. Carefully wet your fingertips in tezu then proceed to spread the rice evenly over the nori. Once spread evenly sprinkle with sesame seeds.

Line up the edge of your nori sheet and the bamboo mat then spread your salmon mix at the bottom end of the nori.

Placing your index and middle fingers in front of your filling to hold it in, position your thumbs under the bamboo mat and roll the mat over to form a tight cylinder.

Begin to roll the mat into tight cylindrical shapes keeping a gentle pressure on the mat. Roll until at the end.

When you have reached the end of your nori sheet, release the mat and lift the Sushi roll off the mat gently.

Using a clean, sharp knife, cut the roll into 6 equal pieces. Clean your knife after each slice.

Remove plastic wrap and Enjoy!

Salmon Sushi Bowl

Sushi rice, salmon, avocado and nori all in a bowl.

Yields: 2 Servings

Time: 15 minutes

Ingredients:

- Sushi rice (1½ cups)
- Salmon (4oz, sashimi grade, thinly sliced, seasoned with salt and lemon)
- Avocado (1/2, thinly sliced)
- Nori (1/4 sheet, cut in strips)
- Sesame Seeds (2 tbsp.)

Directions:

Split your Sushi rice into 2 medium bowls.

Top with your salmon, avocado, and nori strips.

Sprinkle with sesame seeds

Serve and enjoy!

Salmon & Wasabi Sushi Bowl

A spicier version of a salmon sushi bowl.

Yields: 2 Servings

Time: 20 minutes

Ingredients:

- Sushi rice (1½ cups)
- Salmon (4oz, sashimi grade, diced, seasoned with salt and lemon)
- Avocado (1/2, thinly sliced)
- Nori (1/4 sheet, cut in strips)
- Wasabi (5 tbsp.)
- Pickled Ginger (1 tbsp.)
- Soy (2 tbsp.)
- Sesame Seeds (2 tbsp.)

Directions:

Split your Sushi rice into 2 medium bowls.

Top with your salmon, avocado, ginger, soy, wasabi, and nori strips.

Sprinkle with sesame seeds

Serve and enjoy!

Deconstructed Sushi Salad Bowl

All the luxuries of a sushi roll tossed and served in a bowl.

Yields: 2 Servings

Time: 30 minutes

Ingredients:

- Sushi Rice (1 cup)
- Cucumber (4oz, diced)
- Avocado (1/2, diced)
- Carrot (4oz., fine julienne)
- Nori (1/4 sheet, minced)
- Tomato (2 small, diced)
- Rice Vinegar (1 tsp.)
- Salt (1 tsp.)

Directions:

Place all ingredients in a medium bowl, toss, serve and enjoy.

Spicy California Sushi Salad

Spicy and delicious!

Yields: 2 Servings

Time: 30min

Ingredients:

- Sushi rice (1 cup)
- Crab meat (4oz., diced)
- Green Onion (3 tbsp., chopped)
- Carrot (4oz., julienne)
- Nori (1/4 sheet, cut in strips)
- Spicy Mayo (2 tbsp.)

Instructions:

Combine all ingredients in a large bowl. Toss, serve and enjoy.

Conclusion

And there you have it – 30 delicious Sushi recipes for the amateur home cook! Will you go with the classic California roll, or a sushi bowl is more to your liking? Whatever you choose, you'll end up with a delicious meal waiting to be devoured! I hope you had as much fun making these recipes as I've had coming up with them!

About the Author

A native of Indianapolis, Indiana, Valeria Ray found her passion for cooking while she was studying English Literature at Oakland City University. She decided to try a cooking course with her friends and the experience changed her forever. She enrolled at the Art Institute of Indiana which offered extensive courses in the culinary Arts. Once Ray dipped her toe in the cooking world, she never looked back.

When Valeria graduated, she worked in French restaurants in the Indianapolis area until she became the head chef at one of the 5-star establishments in the area. Valeria's attention to taste and visual detail caught the eye of a local business person who expressed an interest in publishing her recipes. Valeria began her secondary career authoring cookbooks and e-books which she tackled with as much talent and gusto as her first career. Her passion for food leaps off the page of her books which have colourful anecdotes and stunning pictures of dishes she has prepared herself.

Valeria Ray lives in Indianapolis with her husband of 15 years, Tom, her daughter, Isobel and their loveable Golden Retriever, Goldy. Valeria enjoys cooking special dishes in her large, comfortable kitchen where the family gets involved in preparing meals. This successful, dynamic chef is an inspiration to culinary students and novice cooks everywhere.

Author's Afterthoughts

Thank you for Purchasing my book and taking the time to read it from front to back. I am always grateful when a reader chooses my work and I hope you enjoyed it!

With the vast selection available online, I am touched that you chose to be purchasing my work and take valuable time out of your life to read it. My hope is that you feel you made the right decision.

I very much would like to know what you thought of the book. Please take the time to write an honest and informative review on Amazon.com. Your experience and opinions will be of great benefit to me and those readers looking to make an informed choice.

With much thanks,

Valeria Ray

Printed in Great Britain
by Amazon